S0-CEJ-196

Simple plants multiply in the seas.

Animals without backbones develop in the seas.

First reptiles appear.
Formation of coal from rotted vegetation begins.

Dinosaurs rule the world.

First apes appear.

First human-looking animal (*Australopithecus*) appears.

Illustrators

Andy Miles pages 24-25
Eric Robson end sheets, pages 12-13, 14-15, 20-21, 28-29 (details)
Chris Shields pages 8-9, 10-11,16-17, 18-19
Tom Stimpson cover, title page, pages 6-7, 28-29 (main illustration)
Peter Visscher pages 22-23, 26-27

Editor Wendy Boase
Designer Matthew Lilly

First published 1985 by Walker Books Ltd,
184-192 Drummond Street, London NW1 3HP

© 1985 Walker Books Ltd

First printed 1985
Printed and bound by L.E.G.O., Vicenza, Italy

British Library Cataloguing in Publication Data
Satchwell, John
Time traveller.–(Young explorers; v.4)
1. Man, Prehistoric–Juvenile literature
I. Title II. Series
930.1 GN744

ISBN 0-7445-0113-X

Contents

In this book:

cm = centimetres
m = metres
kg = kilograms
BC = Before the birth of Christ
AD = Anno Domini (after the birth of Christ)
c. = 'about' (the date)

To read the answer to a quiz, hold a mirror at the right-hand side of the words.

TIME TRAVELLER

By John Satchwell
Consultant Dr Chris Stringer

WALKER BOOKS
LONDON

Walls

Drawing on walls is something people like to do. Sometimes it's patterns, as on wallpaper, or messages sprayed in paint. The first pictures drawn on walls were done 30,000 years ago. The people who drew and painted them were just like us; they had fire, hot dinners and music. But they lived a very different life. For them, shopping meant hunting, and home was a cave where they drew the animals of the chase–bison, reindeer, horses and woolly mammoths.

Imagine you have discovered this cave and in it there is a time tunnel leading back into the past. Why not travel down it to see this mammoth hunt?

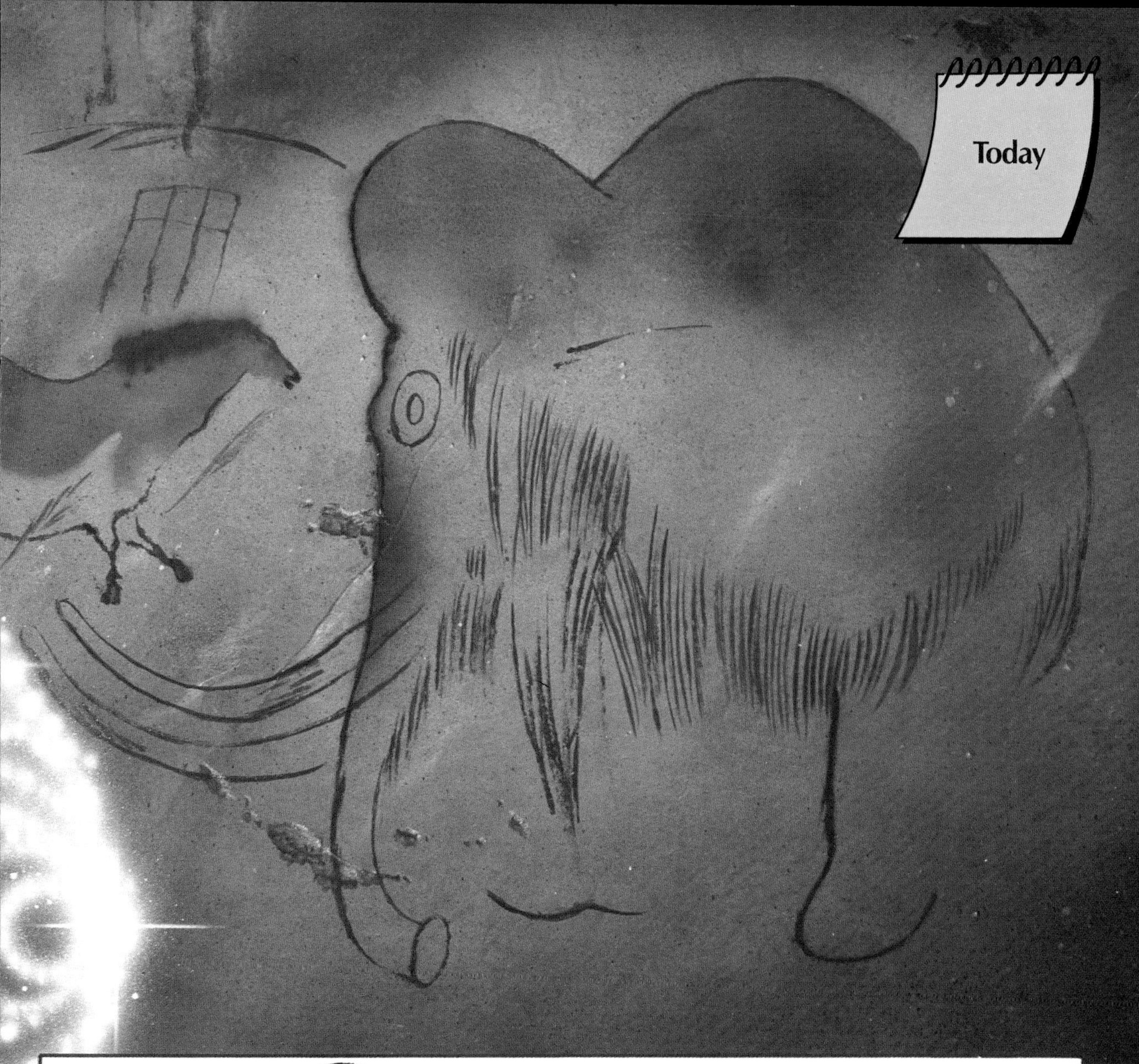

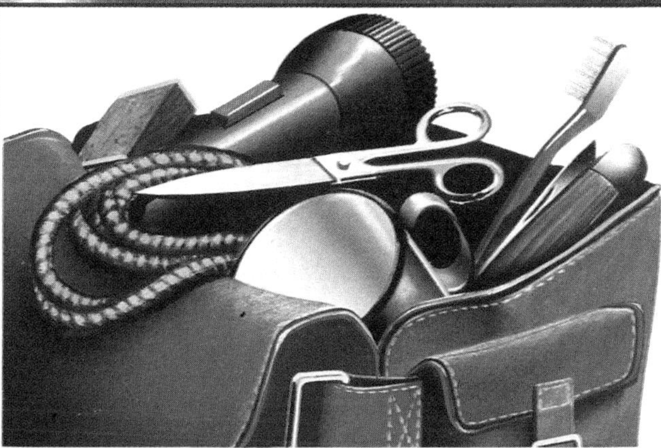

Useful tools
What will you take into the past? Scissors and a penknife, a torch, matches and a rope would be handy. It might be cold, so take a coat, and don't forget a toothbrush. Go . . .

Overshoot

Back through a flicker of days and nights. Over continents and seas. Your target of 30,000 years goes by in a flash. At 70 million years you finally stop. You are in a green, dark swamp, hot and noisy with animal cries. *Tyrannosaurus rex* seems to look at you with evil eyes, but the huge meat-eating dinosaur concentrates on the *Triceratops* feeding in the distance. *Ornithomimus* raids *Tyrannosaurus rex's* eggs while it is not looking. Huge reptiles called *Pteranodon* glide overhead. No human animals ever lived in this age. Here the reptiles rule and danger lurks. Go forward. The mammoth hunt is ahead . . .

. . . *Tyrannosaurus rex*: length 13m; height 6m; weight 7 tonnes. . . *Triceratops*: length 6m; height 3m;

Quiz

Why would *Triceratops* be a more popular guest than *Tyrannosaurus rex*?

Answer

Triceratops would eat up all its vegetables, but T. rex would eat you!

Vegetarian dinosaurs

Triceratops had to chew for hours because early plants were tough and hard to digest. The dinosaurs' fossilized dung shows what plants were like.

weight 8 tonnes; *Ornithomimus*: length 4m; height 2.5m... *Pteranodon*: wing-span 8m...........

Forward

Seen through the speeding years is a procession of fantastic animals. Some look familiar, some seem put together by a mad inventor. For millions of years there is no human-looking animal. Always four legs, never two legs and two arms. Two legs are good for standing up. Hands can hold and use tools. Feet cannot do this.

Eusmilus
Early sabre-toothed cat.

Moropus
Large mammal with huge clawed feet.

Pliohippus
Small one-toed horse.

Ramapithecus
Ape living in Africa, the Near East and Asia 14 to 8 million years ago. Walked and climbed on all fours.

Australopithecus
Human-looking animal! No tools, but hands can grip. Lived in Africa 5 to 2 million years ago.

Pantolambda
Early mammal. Lived mostly in water.

Diatryma
Flesh-eating flightless bird.

Tetonius
Tree-dwelling mammal. Active at night.

Arsinoitherium
Horned mammal; distant relative of elephants.

Dinictis
Distant relative of the cat.

Paraceratherium
Largest land mammal ever known.

Procoptodon
Short-tailed relative of kangaroos.

Look forward!
Just ahead, a bit further down the time tunnel, you can see a kind of half-man, half-ape clutching a stone. Stop and watch…

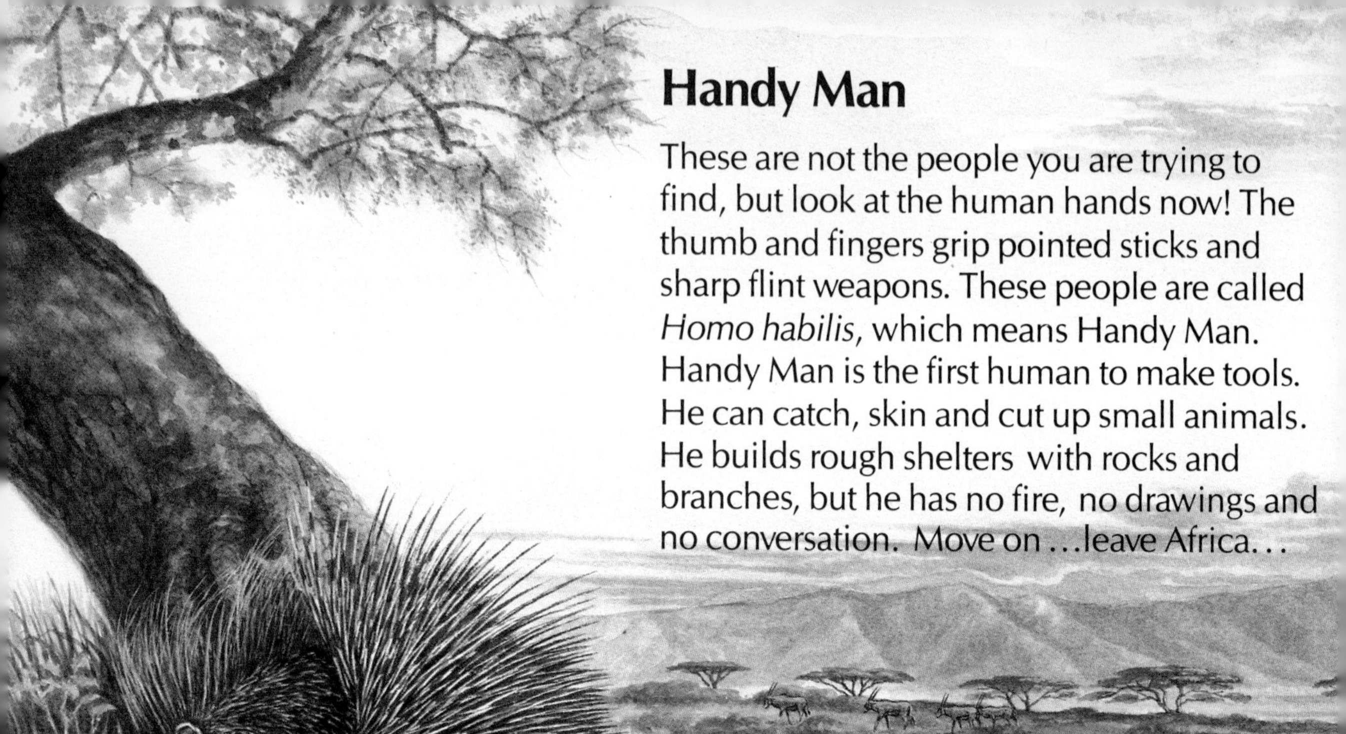

Handy Man

These are not the people you are trying to find, but look at the human hands now! The thumb and fingers grip pointed sticks and sharp flint weapons. These people are called *Homo habilis*, which means Handy Man. Handy Man is the first human to make tools. He can catch, skin and cut up small animals. He builds rough shelters with rocks and branches, but he has no fire, no drawings and no conversation. Move on ...leave Africa...

Choosing a round flint stone as a hammer and one to make into an axe.

The hammer chips off pointed flakes, leaving a sharp edge.

The chopper cuts twigs off a branch. Flakes are for sharpening one end.

......Handy Man lived in Africa 2 to 1.5 million years ago...height 140-160cm; weight 35-50kg;

The digging stick is put to work in the constant search for food.

Grubs, worms and potato-like roots are dug up and eaten raw.

Quiz

Why is Handy Man's hand so handy?

Answer

Fingers and thumb can grip. Try brushing your teeth without using your thumb!

life expectancy 25 years... probably used single words or sounds, but had no proper language......

Upright Man

Here the weather is fine, but with a chill in the air. There are men again, but not the same men–and still not the ones you want, although they stand more upright. They live in huts, speak a sort of language and have fire. This is *Homo erectus*, or Upright Man, at home on the Mediterranean Sea.

For Handy Man, fire was a frightening thing made by lightning strikes and volcanoes. Now it is used for light and heat. In cold weather, fire is important. But Upright Man cannot yet make fire. He must carry it with him and guard it with his life. A box of matches would be magic! Go on…

Untidy man!
The camp is littered with animal bones and broken tools. Upright Man was a good hunter, but not very tidy. His rubbish has become our knowledge.

…Upright Man lived in Europe, Africa and Asia 1 million to 400,000 years ago… height 150-170cm;

400,000 years ago

Quiz

How are we like Upright Man when the weather is cold?

Answer

We wear warm clothes, eat hot food and sit by the fire.

weight 45-55kg; life expectancy 30 years...language helped him to hunt in groups....................

Wise Man's hunt

Steady...50,000 years...40,000...30,000... stop! The cave picture is here in reality. A mammoth, huge and angry, is driven into a marsh. Its size and strength are no match for technology. Fire has frightened it, weapons have wounded it and good brains have planned the marshy trap. The mammoth has muscle, but the men have cleverness. The name *Homo sapiens*, or Wise Man, is given for this cleverness. This is your nearest relative who looks like you. Go home with him, see how he lives...

.......Wise Man lived in Europe, Asia, Africa and Australia...............reached North America by

20,000 years ago............ height 165-185cm; weight 55-75kg; life expectancy 35 years.........

Wise Man's camp

Your first day in Wise Man's camp begins early. It starts with the sun and doesn't stop when darkness falls. The cave is safe, but outside guards must watch for dangerous animals or unfriendly neighbours. It will be hard to survive, although Wise Man has many tools to help him. He can make weapons and digging tools, needles and scrapers. He can even make paints from ground-up rocks mixed with fat. These tools make life easier, and there is more time for thinking. For you, there is time to explore . . .

The fire has faded to a smoking heap. Time to get up. New fire is made by twirling a stick in a hollow stone filled with dry grass.

There is no soap to wash away sleep, and no toothbrushes. Breakfast is fruit, maybe blackberries or wild apples, gathered the day before.

Eggs don't come from the shop, but straight from the nest. Hunting is hard work; egg-collecting is easy. Five-year-olds can do it.

In the afternoon sun, skins are pegged out and the insides scraped clean and smooth. These will make clothing and bedding.

End of the day

After the evening meal there is time for music, painting and story-telling. Only in the safety of the cave, with a full stomach, are such things possible.

Quiz
Why would an air freshener be useful in this cave?

Answer
The cave smells of dirty bodies, dirty teeth, a smoky fire and roasting meat.

Unlucky man

The Wise Man you have met is not the only clever human living at this time. Nearby, you might find another kind of *Homo sapiens* – Neanderthal Man. Shorter and tougher, stronger and hairier, he survives with simpler tools and techniques. He has no music or painting, and little speech, but he buries his dead and puts flowers on the graves.

In the contest for survival, luck is against Neanderthal Man. He scores just as well as the other, true Wise Man for brain size, but not as well for using it. (Look at the score sheets!) In a few years' time, Neanderthal Man will no longer exist.

. . Neanderthal Man lived in Europe 100,000 to 30,000 years ago and in Asia about the same time. . . . .

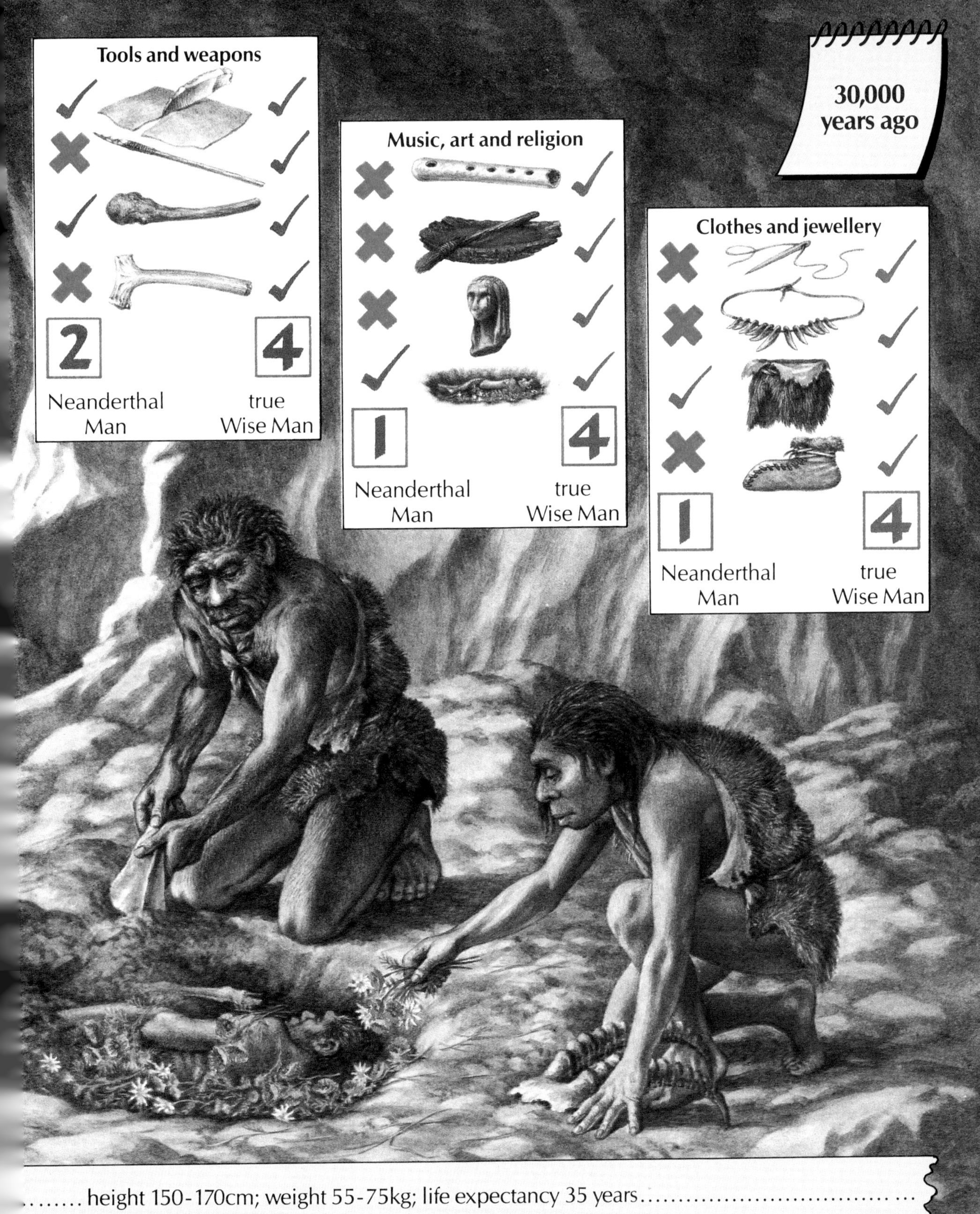

.... height 150-170cm; weight 55-75kg; life expectancy 35 years.................................

Picture show

Wise Man survived all the dangers and we are his children. All he needs to make his life like ours is a few more inventions. Imagine you could show him a bow and arrow, a pot and a wheel. Imagine showing him farming, where animals are tame and food can be grown, or bigger and hotter fires

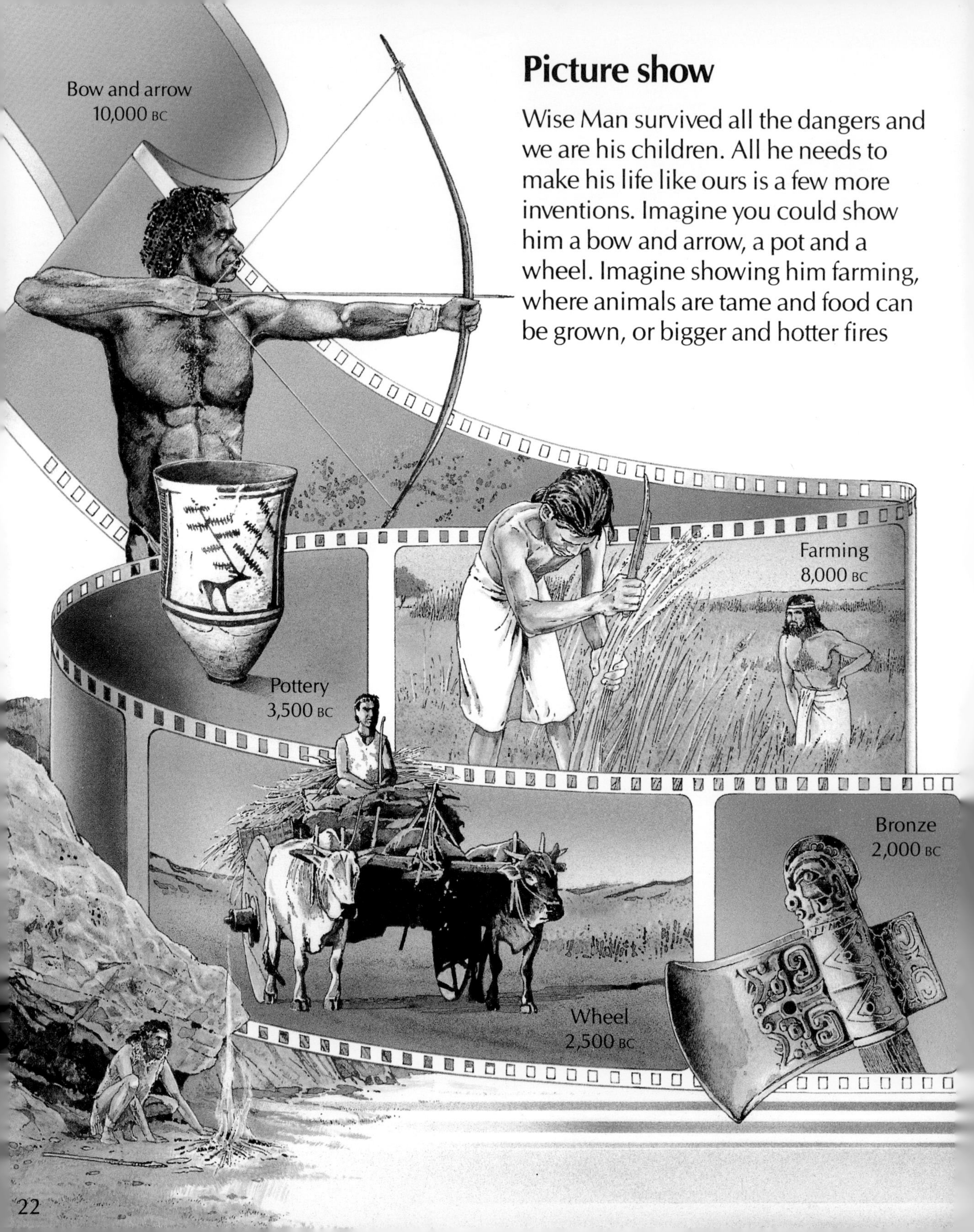

that will melt metals. Metals make better tools than wood or stone. Or show him machines that carry heavier loads than his broad shoulders can. Cleverness and time is all Wise Man needs. But now you must go home, forward through the magic picture show you have given your ancestor...

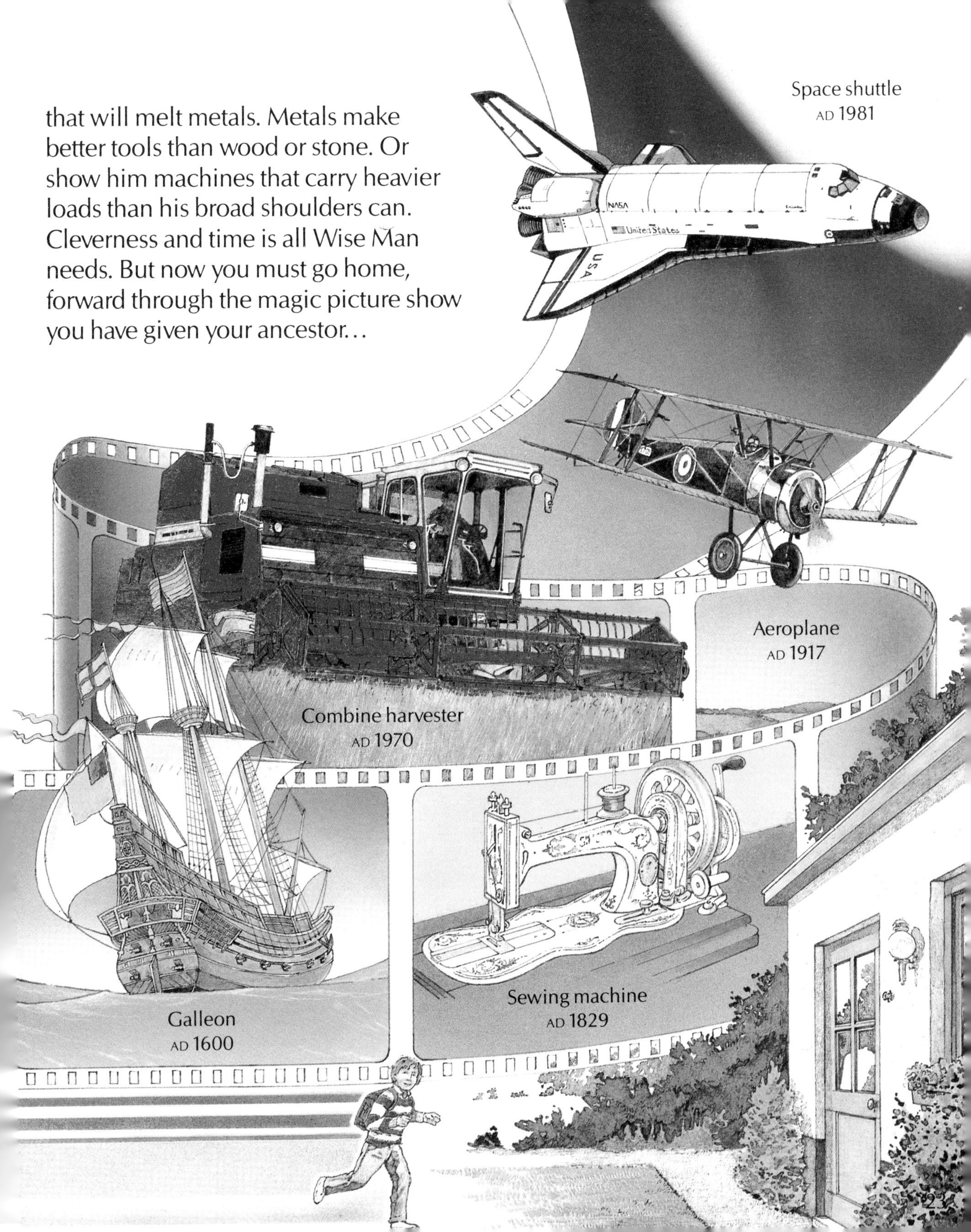

The human race

Life started in the sea and either developed or died out. Play this game to see what might happen in the process of evolution. Use counters and a die. Throw 6 to start.

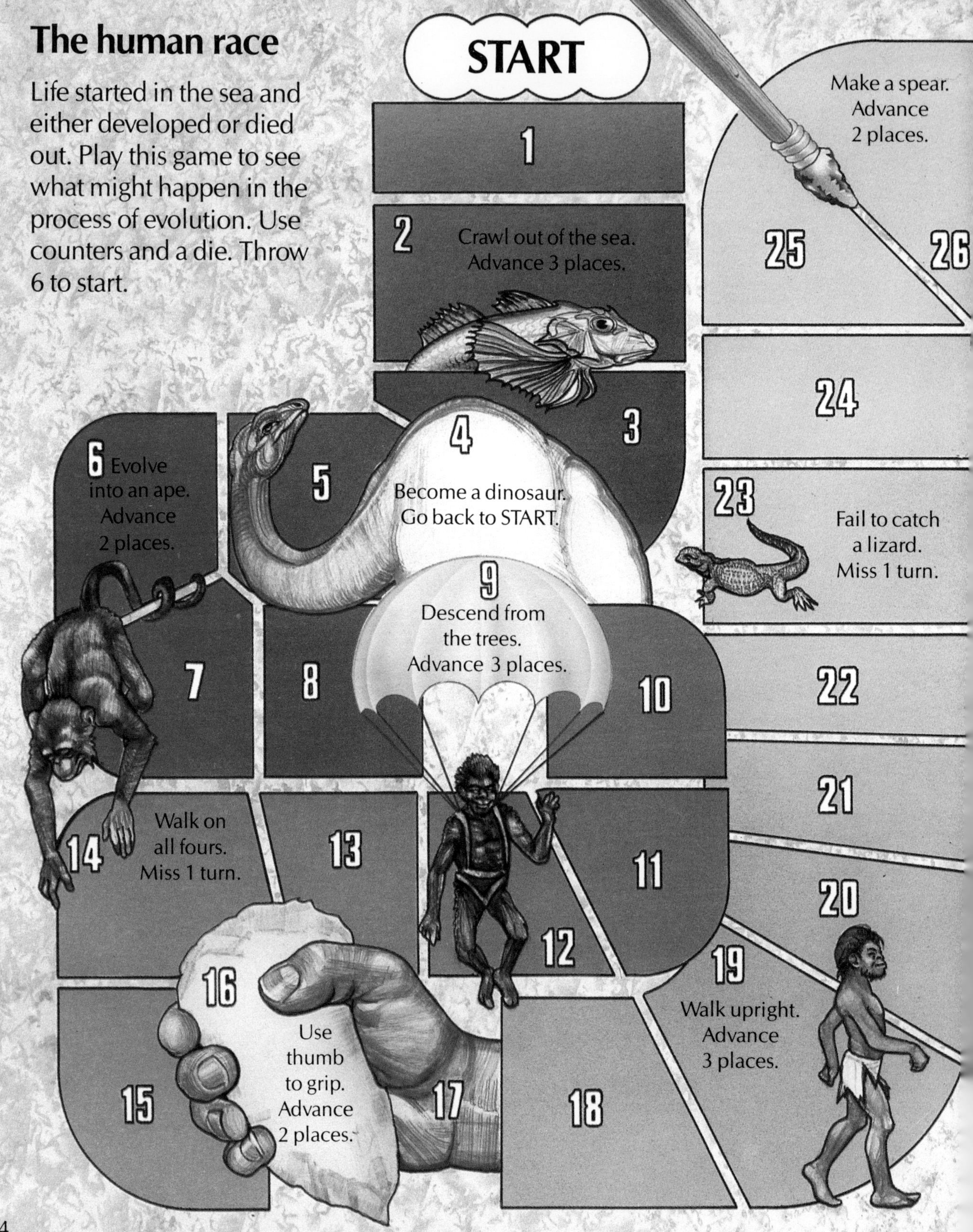

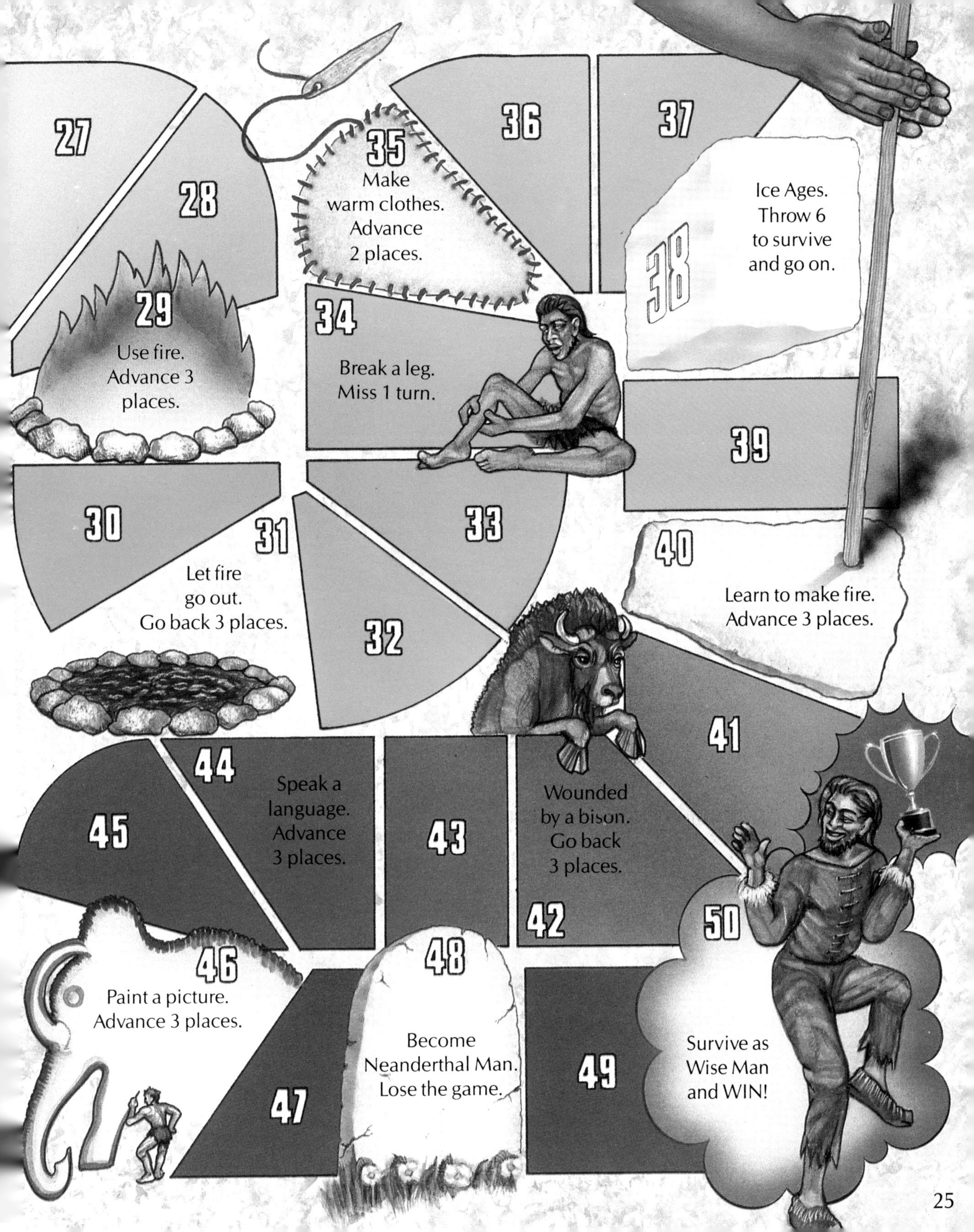
27
28
29
Use fire.
Advance 3
places.
30
31
Let fire
go out.
Go back 3 places.
32
33
34
Break a leg.
Miss 1 turn.
35
Make
warm clothes.
Advance
2 places.
36
37
38
Ice Ages.
Throw 6
to survive
and go on.
39
40
Learn to make fire.
Advance 3 places.
41
42
Wounded
by a bison.
Go back
3 places.
43
44
Speak a
language.
Advance
3 places.
45
46
Paint a picture.
Advance 3 places.
47
48
Become
Neanderthal Man.
Lose the game.
49
50
Survive as
Wise Man
and WIN!

Time warp

Since your journey, you will know a lot more about the past. Test yourself by looking at these 16 pictures. A time warp has caused some things to appear where they don't belong. Five of the pictures are correct. What is wrong in the others?

Tyrannosaurus rex

Answer: humans.

Handy Man

Answer: correct.

Upright Man

Answer: matches.

Upright Man

Answer: bow and arrow.

Neanderthal Man

Answer: watch.

Neanderthal Man

Answer: correct.

Wise Man

Answer: soap.

Australopithecus

Answer: weapon.

Handy Man

Answer: toothbrush.

Handy Man

Answer: dogs and ropes.

Upright Man

Answer: correct.

Wise Man

Answer: correct.

Wise Man

Answer: spectacles.

Neanderthal Man

Answer: flute.

Wise Man

Answer: rubber ball.

Wise Man

Answer: correct.

Mysteries

The story of life on Earth is based on fossils and tools found buried in the ground. The story is not complete, and many mysteries remain unsolved. Why did dinosaurs and mammoths die out? Why did we walk upright? What happened to Neanderthal Man? Could he still be here? In the Himalayas and Rocky Mountains there are stories of half-men, half-apes living near the peaks. In North America they are called Sasquatch or Bigfoot. In Nepal they are called the Yeti. Are they fact or fiction?

Animal puzzles

The oldest fossils of marsupials such as the koala bear have been found in North America. But today most marsupials live in Australia. No one knows how they got from one continent to another.

In 1976 a huge new type of shark was dragged out of the sea. It feeds on shrimps, and is called Megamouth because of the size of its lips and jaws. How many other extraordinary animals remain undiscovered?

Today

Time chart

Rain cools the newly-formed Earth and creates shallow seas.

Volcanic activity forms the earliest known rocks on Earth.

First fishes and first land plants and animals appear.

First mammals appear.

First birds appear.